KINAALDÁ

WE ARE STILL HERE

NATIVE AMERICANS TODAY

KINAALDÁ

A NAVAJO GIRL GROWS UP

Text and Photographs by **Monty Roessel**
With a Foreword by Michael Dorris

Lerner Publications Company ● Minneapolis

Series Editor: Gordon Regguinti
Series Consultants: W. Roger Buffalohead, Juanita G. Corbine Espinosa
Illustrations by Carly Bordeau.

This book is available in two editions:
Library binding by Lerner Publications Company
Soft cover by First Avenue Editions
241 First Avenue North
Minneapolis, MN 55401

ISBN: 0-8225-2655-7 (lib. bdg.)
ISBN: 0-8225-9641-5 (pbk.)

LIBRARY OF CONGRESS CATALOGING-IN-PUBLICATION DATA

Roessel, Monty.
    Kinaaldá : a Navajo girl grows up / text and photographs by Monty
Roessel ; with a foreword by Michael Dorris.
        p.   cm. — (We are still here)
    Includes bibliographical references.
    Summary: Celinda McKelvey, a Navajo girl, participates in the
Kinaaldá, the traditional coming-of-age ceremony of her people.
    ISBN 0-8225-2655-7
    1. McKelvey, Celinda—Juvenile literature. 2. Navajo Indians—
Biography—Juvenile literature. 3. Navajo Indians—Rites and
ceremonies—Juvenile literature. 4. Kinaaldá (Navajo rite)—
Juvenile literature. 5. Puberty rites—New Mexico—Bloomfield—
Juvenile literature. [1. Kinaaldá (Navajo rite) 2. Navajo
Indians—Rites and ceremonies. 3. Indians of North America—
Southwest, New—Rites and ceremonies.] I. Title. II. Series.
E99.N3R597   1993
392'.14—dc20   92-35204
                                                          CIP
                                                          AC

*This book is dedicated to
my wife, Karina, and my four children:
Jaclyn, Bryan, Robert, and Robyn.*

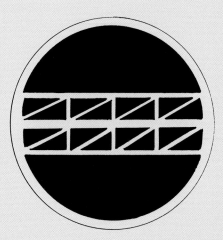

Foreword

by Michael Dorris

How do we get to be who we are? What are the ingredients that shape our values, customs, language, and tastes, that bond us into a unit different from any other? On a large scale, what makes the Swedes Swedish or the Japanese Japanese?

These questions become even more subtle and interesting when they're addressed to distinct and enduring traditional cultures coexisting within the boundaries of a large and complex society. Certainly Americans visiting abroad have no trouble recognizing their fellow countrymen and women, be they black or white, descended from Mexican or Polish ancestors, rich or poor. As a people, we have much in common, a great deal that we more or less share: a recent history, a language, a common denominator of popular music, entertainment, and politics.

But, if we are fortunate, we also belong to a small, more

particular community, defined by ethnicity or kinship, belief system or geography. It is in this intimate circle that we are most "ourselves," where our jokes are best appreciated, our special dishes most enjoyed. These are the people to whom we go first when we need comfort or empathy, for they speak our own brand of cultural shorthand, and always know the correct things to say, the proper things to do.

Kinaaldá provides an insider's view into just such a world, that of the contemporary Navajo people. If we are ourselves Navajo, we will probably nod often while reading these pages, affirming the familiar, approving that this tribal family keeps alive a traditional coming-of-age ceremony. If we belong to another tribe, we will follow this special journey of initiation and education with interest, gaining respect for a way of doing things that's rich and rewarding.

Michael Dorris is the author of *A Yellow Raft in Blue Water, The Broken Cord,* and, with Louise Erdrich, *The Crown of Columbus.* His first book for children is *Morning Girl.*

*I*t was a Friday night in December and 13-year-old Celinda McKelvey lay awake worrying about the weekend. She knew it would be hard work. But this was a time she had dreamed about since she was a little girl. Nothing was going to stop her.

As she tried to go to sleep, all the stories she had heard swirled in her head. She was excited and a little scared. The last thing she remembered before finally falling asleep was an image of herself running. It wasn't a normal run, like when she went for a jog near her home in Bloomfield, New Mexico. This was her Kinaaldá race. It's a race that Celinda begins as a child. When she crosses the finish line, from that moment forward she is an adult.

The Kinaaldá is a coming-of-age ceremony for Navajo girls. It usually takes place when a girl has her first menstrual cycle. The ceremony lasts two to four days.

Navajo people believe that the Kinaaldá is a way for young girls to understand what life will be like when they grow up. As she participates in the Kinaaldá, a girl learns about her culture, and, for the first time, she feels the responsibility of her family. Even as she works side by side with her elders, she knows it is up to her to see that the Kinaaldá is a success.

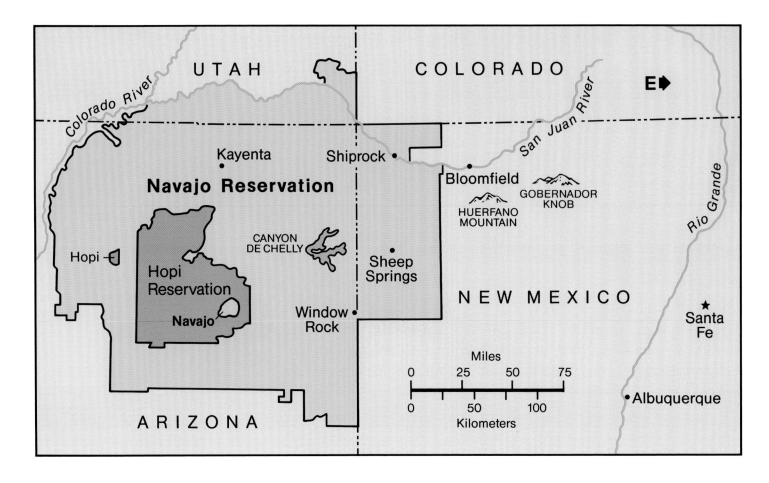

The Navajo Reservation is the largest Indian reservation in the United States; it is almost the size of West Virginia. The land that is sacred to the Navajo people, however, extends beyond the boundaries of the reservation.

The Navajos, or the Diné, as they call themselves (Diné is a Navajo word meaning "the People"), are the largest Indian tribe in the United States. Their population is more than 260,000. The Navajo Reservation spreads across Arizona, New Mexico, and Utah. To drive from one corner of the reservation to another takes more than six hours. The drive takes you through mountains, deserts, and high plateaus. You can see piñon and juniper trees, cactuses, sand dunes, small lakes and mountain streams, as well as dirt roads and highways.

The Kinaaldá ceremony was given to the Navajos by the Holy People. The Holy People are the ones who made the world. Each Holy Person is in charge of certain parts of the universe. Some control the rain and another controls the wind. The Holy People created the Navajos and everything on the earth. To allow the Navajos to prosper, the Holy People gave them ceremonies. The Kinaaldá ceremony so young women could have children. The Enemy Way ceremony for warriors so they would not be haunted by any killing they saw in the war.

A farmer herds sheep near Window Rock. Window Rock is the capital of the Navajo Nation.

The Navajos believe in healing both the mind and the body. If someone hurts his foot, you must also treat his feelings about the injury. Does he feel disappointed? Is he jealous of others who aren't injured? Navajo ceremonies are a way to heal the body and the mind. The most popular ceremony is called the Blessing Way. This ceremony is used to create a balance between the body and the mind. When the body and mind are well, the Navajos call this feeling Hozho, or Harmony. It is the one word that can best sum up Navajo beliefs.

Hundreds of years ago, southwestern Indians carved these petroglyphs (rock carvings) on a cliff in what is now northwestern New Mexico.

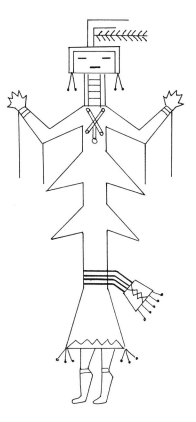

*T*he alarm clock rings at 6:00 Saturday morning. Celinda remains still for a moment, thinking about the day ahead of her. She tries to remember the book she read about the Kinaaldá. She pictures herself wearing her Navajo costume. She sees herself running and grinding corn. Just then her mom, Lucy, opens the bedroom door and shouts: "Hurry up! We're going to be late!"

Celinda doesn't need to be told twice. She jumps out of bed, washes her face, and puts on her clothes. At the foot of her bed is a suitcase. To make sure she wouldn't leave her special clothes and jewelry behind, Celinda packed everything last night.

13

At their home in Bloomfield, New Mexico, Celinda and her sister and parents mix clay to make pottery.

Celinda's father is warming up the van and loading suitcases for the trip to her grandmother's house. Celinda's older sisters, Cecilia and Celeste, are having a hard time waking up. After all, this is a weekend!

Ed, Celinda's dad, gets up early most days, because he's a farmer. Celinda's parents used to be teachers. But her mom always wanted to be an artist. She finally decided to quit her teaching job and start making pottery. After living on the reservation for many years, the family moved off the reservation, to Bloomfield. Now Lucy sells her pots to museums and galleries all over the country.

When everything is ready, the family drives the 100 miles to Grandmother's house in Sheep Springs, New Mexico, on the Navajo Reservation. On the way, Celinda asks her mother to tell the story of the first Kinaaldá.

On the way to Grandmother's house, the family drives by Shiprock, New Mexico, an important landmark for the Navajos.

15

The First Kinaaldá

T he first Kinaaldá was performed for Changing Woman, the most honored of all Navajo Holy People.

One morning at dawn, First Man and First Woman saw a dark cloud over Gobernador Knob. (Gobernador Knob is what it sounds like—a bump on a flat mesa.) When they went to see the cloud, they heard a baby crying within it. First Man found the baby girl who was born of darkness; the dawn was her father. First Man and First Woman raised the child under the direction of the Holy People.

When the girl reached puberty, the Holy People wanted to make a ceremony for her so she could have children. First Woman told the girl, who was called Changing Woman, that she must run four times in the direction of the rising sun. "As you come back you must make the turn sunwise," First Woman said.

To begin the ceremony, Changing Woman's hair was washed with suds made from the root of the yucca plant. Then her hair was tied back.

Next, First Woman decorated a dress for Changing Woman. First she spread out an unwounded buckskin—

one without an arrow hole. On it she placed a piece of turquoise, a bit of white abalone shell, a piece of black obsidian, and a white bead. Then she put white beaded moccasins on the girl's feet. She gave her a skirt and leggings that were also made of white beads. She designed white-bead sleeve fringes and wristlets.

Then First Woman placed her hand on Changing Woman's forehead and moved her hand from Changing Woman's shoulders up over her head. She did this to mold the girl into a woman like herself.

The Holy People said that Changing Woman must make a large cake for the Sun. She was to grind and mix the corn for the batter. When the Sun rose in the east, and after all the prayers were finished, the cake would be given to the Sun. The Sun was given the first piece of cake because he was one of the most powerful of the Holy People. He controlled night and day.

Later, when Changing Woman grew up, the Sun married her. He took her to his home in the western ocean. They had twin boys. These boys became known as Monster Slayer and Child Born for Water.

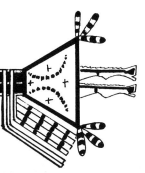

One of Celinda's aunts stands near the fire. Many family members help out during the Kinaaldá.

Suddenly Celinda feels herself bouncing off her seat in the van. "We must be there," she says. "Only Grandmother has a road this bumpy."

As soon as they arrive, there's work to be done. Celinda's father starts a fire and begins to boil barrels full of water. One of her uncles butchers a sheep while another digs a hole in the half-frozen ground. Cecilia and Celeste sift the ground corn, and Lucy cleans the hogan.

A hogan is the traditional home for Navajos. It is an octagonal (eight-sided) building with a stove in the middle and a chimney through the center of the roof. The door always faces the east. The reason is so the sun can shine through the door in the morning and make sure you are not sleeping too much.

Inside a small building next to the hogan, other family members are busy preparing enough food to feed 50 people. Part of the sacredness of a Navajo ceremony is the feeling of family closeness. By the time Celinda's Kinaaldá is over, more than 30 family members and friends will have visited and participated. For the next couple of days, Celinda will be the most important person in the McKelvey family.

"Celinda!" her mother calls. "Come here, we have to get started."

Like many Navajo families, the McKelveys use their hogan mainly for ceremonies.

When Celinda walks into the hogan, she knows the time has come to start her "race." She sits down in front of her mother. They both face the door. Her mother uses a grass brush to fix Celinda's hair. The brush is made of hundreds of tall grass stems tied together. Lucy ties Celinda's hair back with a thin piece of buckskin. Her bangs are left to fall across her face. She is not allowed to wear any makeup. With this simple act of brushing Celinda's hair and tying it back, the Kinaaldá ceremony has begun.

The family sings the first prayer. The prayers for this ceremony are the same as the prayers sung for the first Kinaaldá. They are sung or chanted in Navajo, and they are long—some last more than an hour. This one takes about 30 minutes.

Afterwards, Celinda changes into her Navajo outfit, a black and red woven dress with silver concho shells on the edges. The dress is made just like a Navajo blanket, by weaving wool on a loom. Celinda's mother had the dress made especially for this occasion. Some weavers on the reservation specialize in making certain kinds of rugs. Lucy went to a woman who is known for making "rug dresses." Celinda's dress took more than a month to make.

Heavy turquoise necklaces are then placed around Celinda's neck. Next comes a concho belt that she puts on over a woven sash. Celinda also wears buckskin moccasins that wrap around her calves. This is the way Changing Woman looked when she had her Kinaaldá.

Next, Celinda is asked to lie down on the buckskin and blankets that have been spread on the floor in front of her. In between the blankets and shawls are wallets and car keys, pictures and necklaces. People put these personal items here so that some of the goodness from the prayers will also benefit them.

Navajo ceremonies are as much for the spectators as for the "patient." When a person has a ceremony, he or she is considered the patient, just as when visiting a doctor. For a Kinaaldá, a medicine man serves as doctor.

At the instruction of the medicine man, Celinda's mother begins to "mold" her. This will shape her into a beautiful, strong woman. At first, Lucy places her hands on Celinda softly, then the molding becomes firmer. Celinda doesn't utter a sound as her head is pressed, her eyes softly touched, and her feet rubbed.

Lucy then squeezes her daughter's stomach. "So you don't grow up to be fat," she tells Celinda. Celinda smiles and asks her to squeeze it again. "Just to make sure I stay skinny," she says.

And then people line up to be molded by Celinda. From small babies to grandmothers, they stand in front of her to be touched and shaped by her holy hands.

A woman who complains of bad eyesight asks Celinda to touch her eyes. A man who says his back hurts asks her to squeeze his back. A small person asks her to stretch his neck so he will grow some more. There's a smile on everyone's face. "Maybe this won't be as hard as I thought," Celinda says to herself.

After the molding is finished, Celinda runs out of the hogan toward the east. The people who were molded follow her. As they run, they shout, "Oooyiiee!"

Celinda must run every day of the ceremony—once in the darkness of the morning and again during the afternoon. This is her first run, so she goes only about half a mile. On the next run, Celinda is expected to run farther and faster.

Running toward the east, Celinda almost reaches the highway. She sees several cars and wonders what the people driving by think when they see her. "They probably thought it was some sort of Indian track meet," she tells her mother later with a laugh.

The direction of the run is important. Navajos believe all things begin in the east, where the new day begins. When naming the four directions, Navajos are told to always begin with the east.

If Celinda were to keep running east—about 60 miles farther—she would run into Dzilth-Na-O-Dithle (Huerfano Mountain), the site of the first Kinaaldá. It looks more like a mesa than a mountain. It's a rugged landscape of tall cliffs and scarce vegetation. From Celinda's grandmother's house, just the tip of the mountain can be seen.

The whole area around Huerfano Mountain is sacred to the Navajos. It is here, Navajo stories say, that the People came up from the underworld. This is one reason the Navajos call the earth Mother Earth. It gave birth to Diné, the People.

The earth is central to Navajo culture. The plants, animals, and sky are alive. If the right words are spoken, their voices can be heard. If something is taken from the earth, something must also be returned.

These days, many Navajo children are taught Navajo language in school.

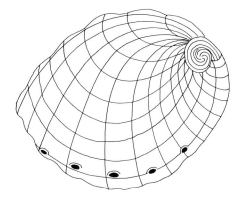

*I*n the 1950s and 1960s, the Kinaaldá ceremony almost died. It was a time when most Navajo children were taken away from their families by the United States government and sent to boarding schools. At these schools, Navajos were punished for speaking their own language. The only time they were allowed to come home was for the summer. The children did not spend much time with the elders who knew the Kinaaldá and other ceremonies. As a result, the ceremonies were performed less and less often. Young girls were growing up without having the Kinaaldá. Some families forgot how to perform it.

Luckily, things have changed. Children are no longer sent to boarding schools. Now many schools on the reservation teach Navajo language and culture. About three-fourths of Navajo people speak the language. In recent years—and no one is sure exactly why—families started to hold ceremonies again. There was a rebirth of Navajo pride. Pretty soon the Kinaaldá became one of the most popular Navajo ceremonies.

Ceremonies like the Kinaaldá help young people understand what it means to be both an American Indian and a Navajo. The Kinaaldá is a way for young Navajos to share the culture of past generations. Even now there are so many questions that Navajos must ask themselves about their identity. They wonder whether they should speak Navajo or English in public, whether to see a doctor or a medicine man or both, and whether girls should wear their hair in a traditional bun.

"What is a Navajo?" is a hard question for a young girl to answer. It is especially hard if you live off the reservation, as Celinda does. But in her heart, Celinda knows she is Navajo. A ceremony like the Kinaaldá makes her proud of who she is.

During the ceremonies, young people learn from their elders, and in this way the Navajo traditions stay alive.

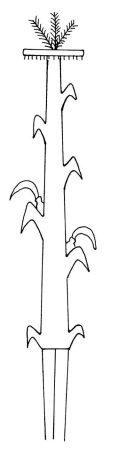

After Celinda has completed her first run, she returns to the hogan to prepare the cake. Much of a Kinaaldá ceremony centers around the making of a cake in the earth. Although Kinaaldá is the name of the ceremony, most people just say "Celinda is making her cake."

First, a hole about 4 feet wide and 11 inches deep is dug in the ground outside the hogan. A bigger hole creates extra work in preparing the cake, and if the hole is smaller it's said that the young girl will have too easy a time. Most of the measuring is done with a shovel. It is not an exact science. The usual instructions are to "make a hole about the length of a shovel and as deep as your elbow." Since there are many different sizes of shovels and arms, no two holes are identical.

Celinda's cousins watch as an aunt boils water for the cake batter.

Next, wood is thrown into the hole and a fire is started inside it. The fire heats the walls and bottom of the hole and hardens the earth. Since the ground is mostly sand, it needs to "cook" a little before the cake batter is poured in. Otherwise, the walls of the hole would collapse and sand would get into the cake.

While the men are preparing the "oven" in the ground, Celinda is inside the hogan getting the batter ready. The recipe is simple: cornmeal, hot water, and a sweetener made from wheat. Baking soda keeps the batter from getting lumpy.

Celinda sticks her hands into the batter and starts to mix it. At first it seems pretty easy. But when she asks if she's almost done, her aunt tells her that she still has to mix the whole pile of cornmeal behind her. Celinda thinks she must be kidding. But then another bucket comes, and another. Her arms and back grow sore from stirring.

Several women begin to help Celinda. They grab their stirring sticks and sit on the floor of the hogan as they stir. The stirring sticks are made of 8 to 12 greasewood sticks tied together. These sticks are sacred to the women. They received them during their own Kinaaldás, many years ago. The women treasure their sticks for their whole lives.

"In the old days," Celinda's aunt tells her, "we didn't have a machine to grind the corn. We had to grind all of the cornmeal on a grinding stone. No one helped us. You're lucky."

For the most part, the Kinaaldá ceremony has remained the same through many centuries. But, like most Indians, Navajos have had to adapt to a changing world. These days, most of the corn is ground at a mill. A girl must still use a grinding stone to grind part of the corn, though.

Another change is that some families, like the McKelveys, shorten the ceremony to two days to fit into a girl's school schedule. The Kinaaldá traditionally lasts four days.

Ground corn is a very important part of the Kinaaldá ceremony. Celinda blesses each batch of cornmeal before using it.

Christine lets Celinda know if she's made a mistake. The corn husks have to be sewn perfectly.

After spending nearly an hour at the grinding stone, Celinda is sent to the sewing corner. It is time to sew corn husks together to make a crust-cover for the cake. The task isn't as easy as it sounds.

"No! Not that way. That's upside-down," Celinda's aunt yells. "All the husks must face clockwise, and they must be sewn together so they flow in one direction." Celinda's aunt, Christine Allen, has been helping girls from the Sheep Springs area make their cakes since before Celinda was born.

When she is finished, Celinda holds up the four-foot round crust-cover. This will keep dirt out of the cake and prevent it from burning. Her aunt smiles and says, "Very pretty. Now make another one just like it."

After nearly three hours of grinding corn, mixing batter, and sewing corn husks, the preparations are almost complete. Now, cornmeal is placed in a basket. Celinda walks out of the hogan to where the fire has been burning over the hole in the earth. One of the uncles puts out the fire and lines the hole with paper bags and one of the corn-husk covers. Then he pours the batter into the ground, and the second corn-husk cover is then placed on top of the cake.

Opposite: *First the fire is cleared, then the bottom crust cover is laid down. Finally the batter is poured in.* Above: *Celinda carries a basket of cornmeal to sprinkle on top of the batter as a blessing.*

"Where is Celinda?" Lucy calls out.

"Right behind you," Celinda answers.

"It's time to bless the cake," her mother says.

With the basket of cornmeal in her left hand, Celinda takes a handful of cornmeal in her right hand and sprinkles it across the cake in a clockwise motion. She then grabs another handful of cornmeal and sprinkles a little toward the east side of the cake. She repeats the action toward the south and west and ends with the north. With a final handful of cornmeal she circles the edges of the cake, making sure to sprinkle in a clockwise direction.

Friends and family members bless the cake for themselves and for Celinda.

One by one, the people who have gathered around Celinda copy her actions and bless the cake. When they are done, the basket of cornmeal is empty.

Paper bags are laid over the corn-husk crust and dirt is scattered across the hole. The fire is relighted. The cake will cook throughout the night.

Tomorrow the ceremony will be over, but first Celinda has to make it through a night of prayers. She must stay awake all night as prayers are sung. Each prayer introduces Celinda to the Holy People, in the hope that they will protect Celinda on her journey through life. Because the prayers are sacred, participants must not recite them outside of a ceremony.

Celinda stands by the fire that was built over the cake. The fire will burn through the night as the prayers are sung.

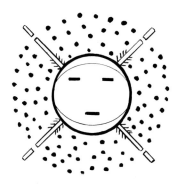

As the day turns into night, pickup trucks and cars arrive at Celinda's grand-mother's hogan. Word has been passed around the small community that a ceremony is being held. A blanket in the doorway of the hogan sym-bolizes the ceremony within. Parents enter the hogan while children bundle up in sleeping bags in the back of campers. The people inside the hogan will help the medicine man pray during the night.

Celinda stands next to the fire that is cooking her cake. She tries to keep warm as she waits for the praying to begin. To fight the cold, people huddle around the fire. A neighbor, Lee Joe, pulls up a chair next to the fire. He holds a shovel. It's his job to make sure the fire does not burn out or get too hot. "I always wanted to be a baker," he jokes to Celinda.

An uncle appears and tells Celinda it's time to go inside. She enters the hogan, walking clockwise around the fireplace. To go counterclockwise is disrespectful to the Holy People. She sits next to the medicine man on the west side of the hogan, facing the door. It is time to start the prayers.

The fire burns brightly in the fireplace, making shadows dance against the walls of the hogan. All that can be heard is the hum of people talking quietly and the crackle of the fire.

And then the chanting begins. At first, only the medicine man prays. Then, one by one, other voices join in. At last, there is a chorus of prayers.

Through the night Celinda is required to sit with her legs stretched out in front of her and her back straight. This is probably the most grueling part of the ceremony. After a while she starts looking forward to running again, just to be able to stretch her legs and relax her back.

Shortly before dawn, she gets her wish. The hogan grows quiet. The door is opened and the blanket drawn back. Celinda leaves the hogan and begins to run. Suddenly people in pickup trucks and cars open their doors and run after Celinda. In the darkness, the only sounds are the pounding of cowboy boots and tennis shoes and the high-pitched "Oooyiiee" of young and old runners.

A little while later, wrapped in a colorful blanket, Celinda runs back past the fire and into the hogan. About 15 runners follow her. The door shuts and it is quiet. The prayers are over.

On the horizon glows the faint light of dawn. The emerging dawn means that Celinda's childhood is almost over. As the runners rest inside the hogan, Celinda's parents and aunts work quickly to cut the cake outside.

In the morning, Celinda's mother and aunts get ready to cut the cake.

43

The wind starts to blow, so they prop up pieces of plywood to shield against the wind. The paper bags are removed from the oven and Lucy slides a knife into the cake to see if it is cooked.

"Perfect," she says. "It's better than mine was."

Celinda is relieved. It is believed that if the cake is still gooey when the sun rises, the young girl will have a hard life. Lucy cuts the cake into small pieces. The center of the cake—the most sacred part—will be given to the most special people at the ceremony.

Celinda takes a turn at cutting the cake.

Now only two tasks remain—the last molding, and eating the cake. As Celinda stands in the doorway, her aunts and uncles lay the blankets and buckskin before her. Once again, keys and lucky charms are placed between the blankets. This will be the last chance to share in the blessing of the Kinaaldá.

After the last person is molded, everyone returns inside to eat the cake. The hogan is packed with people. Celinda hand-delivers every piece of cake. Each time she gives someone a piece, she says, "Thank you for coming." Celinda's grandmother and the medicine man each receive a piece from the center.

Pretty soon, the cake is all gone. Celinda will eat from her family's portion. Then she sits down and rests—finally.

Celinda brings some of the cake into the hogan. Inside, the pieces are stacked up, ready to be given out.

The early morning light enters the window, creating a golden glow in the hogan. Celinda herself is glowing with pride. Her aunts tease her, but their words aren't as sharp as they were yesterday. She is one of them now. She has finished the race.

"I can't believe that I've done it," Celinda says. "I kept telling myself, you can't quit. I know I don't look any different, but I feel different. I feel like a Navajo. Just like my mom and my aunts and my grandmother."

Word List

abalone—mollusks that have flat, somewhat spiral-shaped white shells

Diné *(dee-NEH)*—Navajo word meaning "the People," which Navajos use to describe themselves

hogan *(ho-GAHN)*—eight-sided buildings that are traditional Navajo homes

Holy People—Navajo spiritual beings

Kinaaldá *(kee-nahl-DAH)*—a coming-of-age ceremony for Navajo girls

mesa—a flat-topped hill or mountain

Navajos—American Indian people who live in the Southwest

obsidian—black volcanic glass that looks like rock

reservation—an area of land that Indian people kept through agreement with the United States government

For Further Reading

Between Sacred Mountains: Navajo Stories and Lessons from the Land. Vol. II, SUN TRACKS. Tucson, AZ: Sun Tracks and the University of Arizona Press, 1982.

Iverson, Peter. *The Navajos.* New York: Chelsea House Pub., 1990.

Roessel, Robert A., Jr. *Pictorial History of the Navajo.* Rough Rock, AZ: Navajo Curriculum Center, Rough Rock Demonstration School, 1980.

Roessel, Ruth, ed. *Stories of Traditional Navajo Life and Culture.* Tsaile, AZ: Navajo Community College Press, 1977.

Roessel, Ruth. *Women in Navajo Society.* Rough Rock, AZ: Navajo Resource Center, Rough Rock Demonstration School, 1981.

William, Terry T. *Pieces of White Shell: A Journey to Navajoland.* Albuquerque: University of New Mexico Press, 1987.

About the Contributors

Monty Roessel is a Navajo photographer and writer who specializes in contemporary Native Americans, especially the Navajos. Upon graduation from the University of Northern Colorado, he worked for various newspapers as a photographer and editor before becoming a freelance photojournalist. His photographs have appeared in many magazines, including *Time, Newsweek, Arizona Highways, The New York Times Magazine,* and *Sports Illustrated.* Roessel's work is also included in books such as *Baseball in America, Photographing Arizona, Native America,* and *Beyond the Mythic West.* When not on assignment, Roessel works on a personal project documenting, from a Navajo's perspective, contemporary Navajo life.

Series Editor **Gordon Regguinti** is a member of the Leech Lake Band of Ojibway. He was raised on Leech Lake Reservation by his mother and grandparents. His Ojibway heritage has remained a central focus of his professional life. A graduate of the University of Minnesota with a B.A. in Indian Studies, Regguinti has written about Native American issues for newspapers and school curricula. He served as editor of the Twin Cities native newspaper *The Circle* for two years and is currently executive director of the Native American Journalists Association. He lives in Minneapolis and has six children and one grandchild.

Series Consultant **W. Roger Buffalohead**, Ponca, has been involved in Indian Education for more than 20 years, serving as a national consultant on issues of Indian curricula and tribal development. He has a B.A. in American History from Oklahoma State University and an M.A. from the University of Wisconsin, Madison. Buffalohead has taught at the University of Cincinnati, the University of California, Los Angeles, and the University of Minnesota. Currently he teaches at the American Indian Arts Institute in Santa Fe, New Mexico. Among his many activities, Buffalohead is a founding board member of the National Indian Education Association and a member of the Cultural Concerns Committee of the National Conference of American Indians. He lives in Santa Fe.

Series Consultant **Juanita G. Corbine Espinosa**, Dakota/Ojibway, is the director of Native Arts Circle, Minnesota's first statewide Native American arts agency. She is first and foremost a community organizer, active in a broad range of issues, many of which are related to the importance of art in community life. In addition, she is a board member of the Minneapolis American Indian Center and an advisory member of the Minnesota State Arts Board's Cultural Pluralism Task Force. She was one of the first people to receive the state's McKnight Human Service Award. She lives in Minneapolis.

Illustrator **Carly Bordeau** is a member of the Anishinabe Nation, White Earth, Minnesota. She is a freelance graphic designer, illustrator, and photographer and the owner of All Nite Design and Photography. Carly graduated from the College of Associated Arts in St. Paul with a B.A. in Communication Design. She lives in St. Paul.